nickelodeon

PAW PATROL™

CW01583248

EARLY LEARNING WORKBOOK

FIRST SPELLING

Ages 4–5

SCHOLASTIC

Developed in conjunction with Charlotte Raby, educational consultant

Scholastic Children's Books,
Euston House, 24 Eversholt Street,
London NW1 1DB, UK

A division of Scholastic Ltd
London ~ New York ~ Toronto ~ Sydney ~ Auckland
Mexico City ~ New Delhi ~ Hong Kong

Published in the UK by Scholastic Ltd, 2019

ISBN 978 1407 19288 8
Printed in Malaysia
2 4 6 8 10 9 7 5 3 1

Papers used by Scholastic Children's Books are made from wood grown in sustainable forests.

www.scholastic.co.uk

Hello, Pups!

The PAW Patrol pups are here to help you learn to spell while having fun! Soon you will be able to spell words with different letter sounds, words with long and short vowel sounds and tricky words, too. Practise spelling the words taught in schools and look out for the special reward stickers!

The answers are on pages 44 to 47.

PAW Patrol – here to help!

Ready for Action!

Add the missing pup stickers.

Say each pup's name out loud, then write the missing letter. Remember, names start with a capital letter.

Chase

Marshall

Everest

Rocky

Rubble

Skye

Tracker

Zuma

Write your name here.

The Alphabet and Capital Letters

Here are all the letters of the alphabet in order. Say the letter sounds out loud.

When you come to a character, circle the capital letter at the start of their name.

a A
apple

b B
ball

c C
Cali

d D
duck

e E
Everest

f F
fish

g G
goat

h H
hat

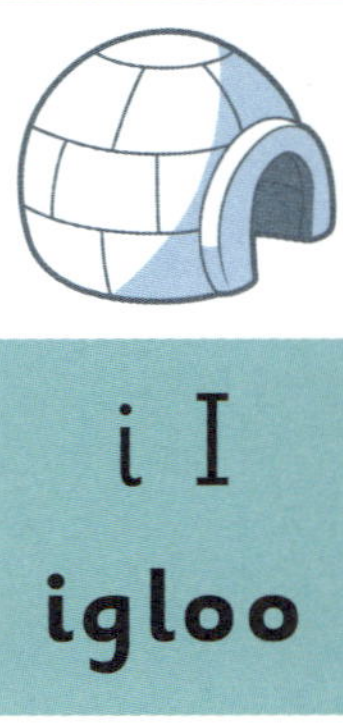

i I
igloo

j J
jug

k K
Katie

l L

lamp

m M

Marshall

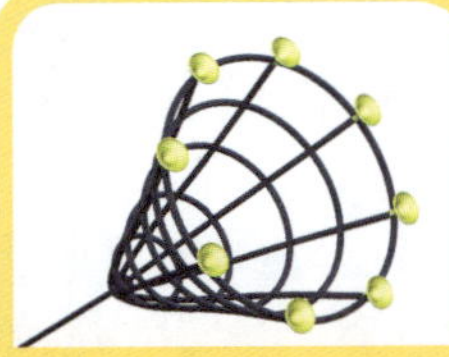

n N

net

o O

orange

p P

PupPad

q Q

quick

r R

Rubble

s S

snow

t T

train

u U

umbrella

v V

van

w W

Wally

x X

box

y Y

yo-yo

z Z

Zuma

Try to say the letter sounds without an 'uh' at the end, so 'sss' rather than 'suh'.

Short Vowel Sounds

There are five vowels in the alphabet.
Say the short vowel sounds out loud:

a e i o u

Write a vowel to make a word that matches the picture each time.

1 

h _ t

2 

b _ x

3 

b _ g

4 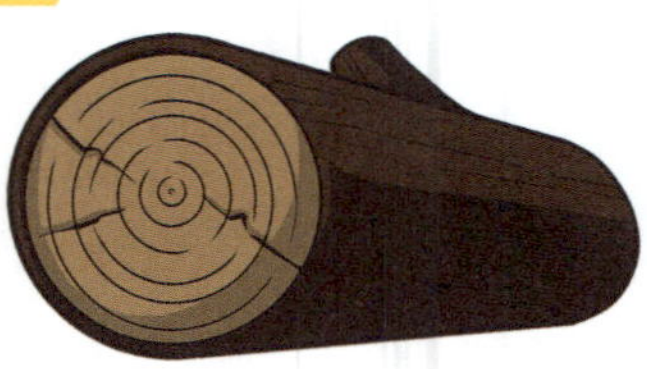

l _ g

5 

b _ n

6 

b _ t

This time add the short vowel sounds to finish the sentences.

Rubble can
d_g it!

No job is too
b_g, no p_p
is too small!

Cali the c_t
cannot st_p!

P_t it in the b_n!

Let's Spell Action Words

The PAW Patrol pups are ready to play!
Here are lots of things they can do.

Say the words out loud,
then trace them.

jump run kick

sprint hop skip

bend stamp

Choose the best word to finish these sentences.

jump kick catch sit

1  Rocky can ....

2  Will Chase .... it?

3  Skye can .... it.

4  Jump, Marshall, ... !

Pup Fun

Read the words in the box, then use them to label the picture.

bed	book	brush
ted	bowl	bath

Digraphs

A digraph is when two letters are blended together to make one sound. Say the sounds out loud.

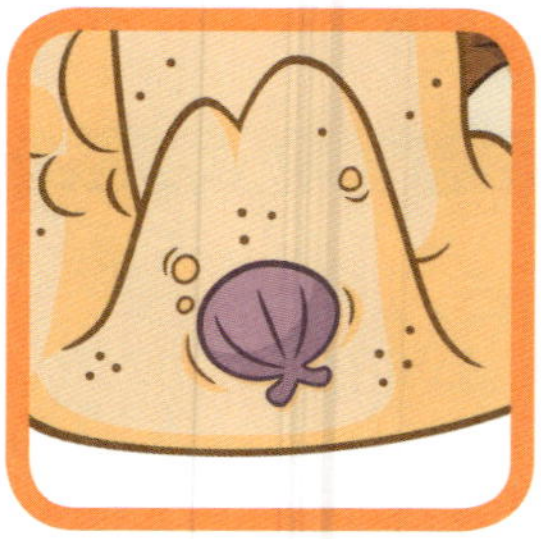

sh

th

ch

ll

Now trace the words below.

shell bath

chair hill

ng

qu

ck

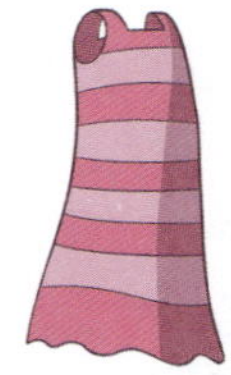

ss

ff

Trace these words too.

truck ring

dress

quick off

Words with 2, 3 and 4 Sounds

Read the words below and say each sound. Then draw lines to match the words to the correct number of sounds. One has been done for you.

am

top

2 sounds

on

it

3 sounds

4 sounds

cat

sun

help

Add a sticker when you've matched all the words.

Two letters can make one sound:

duck thump chop stop

Try reading the new words below and saying the sounds.
Then match the words to the correct number of sounds.
One has been done for you.

jump shop

3 sounds

lick chin

4 sounds

lift

tent

push

When you've finished, add a sticker.

Tricky Words

These words all have a tricky bit that can't be read by sounding out the letter. The tricky bit is circled. Read these words out loud together, then practise spelling the words.

the

he

to

she

no

we

go

me

into

be

Say the tricky words out loud,
then add the stickers.

Rainbow Words

Write the number words from one to seven in rainbow colours.

Start with number one at the top of the rainbow.

one two three four

five six seven

Add a Skye sticker when you have finished!

Alien Words

An alien has landed in Adventure Bay!

Say the words out loud, then add stickers to show only the real words.

grig

pip

kiff

jump

whizz

vap

meck

bigh

hug

spin

Dot and Dash Words

Say the words out loud. Then draw lines to match the words to the pictures.

frog

back

net

truck

zip

van

shell

log

chick

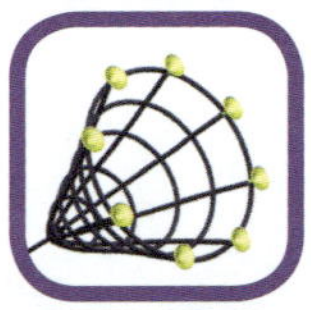

Draw a dot under each letter that makes one sound (**phonemes**). Draw a dash under two letters that make one sound (**digraphs**). The first word has been done for you.

	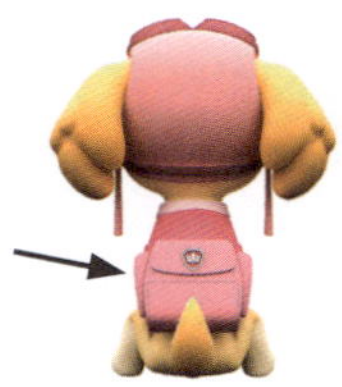	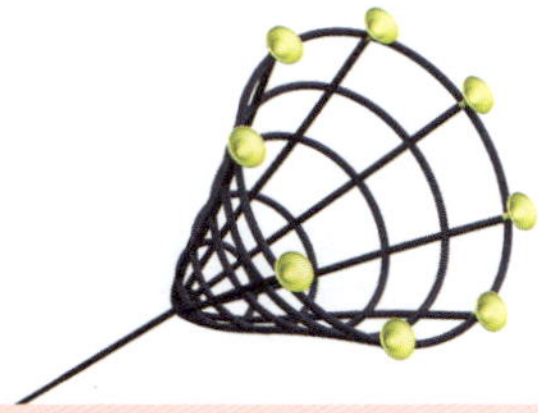
frog	back	net

truck	zip	van

shell	log	chick

Spelling Words with Two Syllables

Look at the pictures, then draw lines to make animal words.

	spi	bit
	rab	en
	zeb	ra
	chick	der

Now draw lines to make some yummy food words.

	mush	corn
	pop	room
	tur	rot
	car	nip

This time draw a circle around the word that is correctly split into two syllables.

1		hel met	helm et
2		tra iners	train ers
3		han dbag	hand bag
4		jac ket	jack et
5		jet pack	jetpa ck
6		skate board	ska teboard
7		toyb ox	toy box
8		footb all	foot ball

Let's Sort Sounds

These words all have an **a** sound in them. Read the words, then tick whether each word has a **long a** sound or a **short a** sound.

word	long a sound	short a sound
wait		
bang		
tail		
aim		
black		
stamp		
sail		
train		
hand		
cat		

Colour in the pup treats to show how many words you got right.

1 2 3 4 5 6 7 8 9 10

This time sort the **long e** and **short e** words.
Say the words out loud, then tick the right box each time.

word	long e sound	short e sound
peg		
sleep		
bed		
leg		
deep		
feel		
pen		
keep		
see		
sheep		

Colour in a paw print to show how many words you got right.

1 2 3 4 5
6 7 8 9 10

Ruff-ruff Rescue

Are you ready for a ruff-ruff rescue?
Add the long vowel sounds to reveal the words,
then follow the clues to save the day!

Write the words. Choose: **ee** or **ai**.

ee ai

1. Start at the gr_ _n tr_ _.
2. Follow the direction of Rocky's t_ _l.
3. What can Chase s_ _? It's a b_ _.
4. Head towards the tr_ _n.
5. Cr_ _p past one pup fast asl_ _p.
6. Well done! You have found the lost sh_ _p.

Place your sticker here
if you saved the day!

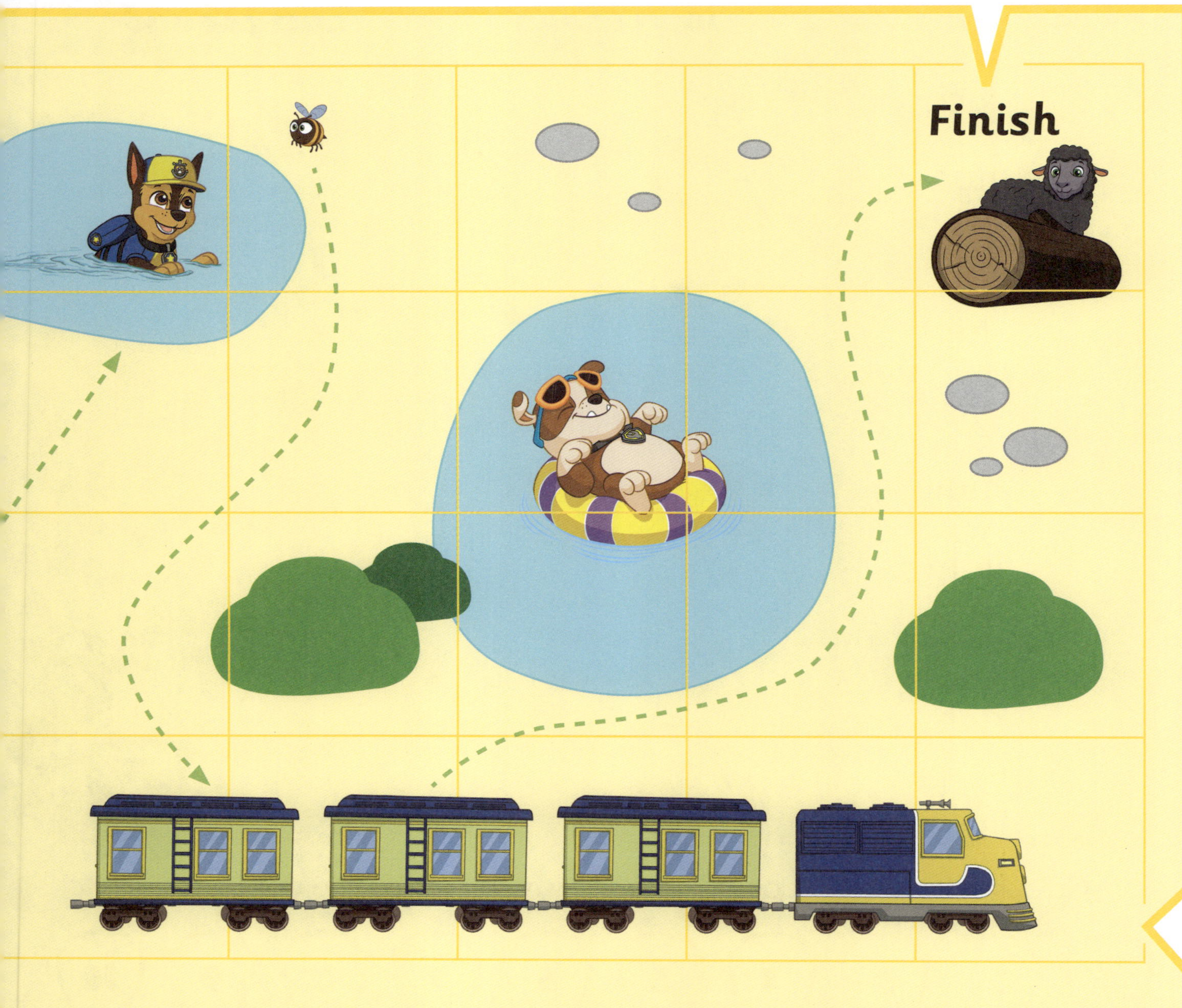

Let's Sort Sounds

Say these words with an **i** sound, then sort them into the right boxes.

word	long i sound	short i sound
kick		
night		
fish		
hill		
fit		
high		
light		
bin		
right		
sigh		

Colour in the pup badges to show how many words you got correct.

1 2 3 4 5 6 7 8 9 10

Do these words have a **long o** or a **short o** sound?
Say the words out loud, then tick the right box each time.

word	long o sound	short o sound
dot		
job		
sock		
road		
goat		
pocket		
float		
goat		
hot		
coat		

Colour in a star for each word you got right.

1 2 3 4 5 6 7 8 9 10

The Alphabet

Farmer Yumi is picking carrots, but some have gone missing.

Use your stickers to plant some more carrots in the correct order of the alphabet.

Reading Sentences

How well do you know the PAW Patrol pups? Read the words out loud. Then find the right word to finish the sentence for each pup.

wet | Green | ruff | swing | dig

1 Let's .... it!

2 .... means go!

3 I can .... it!

4 Ready, set, get .... !

5 Time for a ruff-.................... rescue!

More Vowel Sounds

Here are some new words. Some have a long vowel sound, some have a short vowel sound. Read them out loud, then sort them into the right boxes.

word	long oo sound	short u sound
roof		
food		
mud		
bucket		
moon		
sun		
bug		
zoom		
cool		
pup		

Colour in the pup treats to show how many words you got right.

1 2 3 4 5 6 8 7 9 10

The words in each row all have the same long vowel sound, except for one. Circle the word that sounds different each time.

ar

 car

 jar

 star

 train

 barn

or

 corn

 moon

 worn

 fork

 shorts

ow

 cow

 brown

 float

 down

 owl

More Tricky Words

All these words have a tricky bit that can't be sounded out. The tricky bit is circled. Write the words again, spelling the letters out loud.

you	was
they	said
all	have
are	like
my	so
her	the

Rubble on the Double!

Rubble has a rocky load to shift today! Use the coloured dots to help you colour in the picture.

brown yellow black grey

Cover the colour words above, then spell them again below.

Let's Write Plurals

Plural means 'more than one'. When we have more than one of something we usually add the letter **s** to the end of the word.

rabbit

bird

owl

cat

frog

chicken

Trace over these plural words, then write them out again.

rabbits

birds

owls

cats

frogs

chickens

Spelling Practice

These words all have two syllables and one long vowel sound.

Draw lines to match the words with the pictures.

hardhat	
tugboat	
sweetcorn	
balloon	
trainers	
toolbox	
lightbulb	
rainbow	

Trace the words, then write them out again.
Circle the long vowel sound in each word.

Remember: the long vowel sounds here are
ai ee igh oo.

trainers

balloon

rainbow

sweetcorn

hardhat

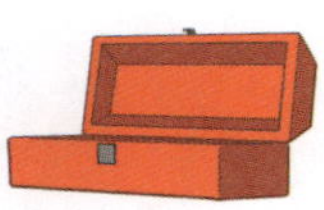
toolbox

tugboat

lightbulb

Here Are All the Things I Can Do

Stick a paw print sticker next to each skill you have learned.

Handwriting

I can...

- hold a pencil in the correct position.
- form all the letters of the alphabet correctly.

Reading and Spelling

I know...

- that letters make sounds.
- the order of the alphabet.

I can...

- blend sounds to read words.
- read and spell words with the long vowels: ***ai ee igh oa oo ar or ow***.
- read and spell words with more than one syllable.

Tricky Words

I can read and spell the tricky words:

the	no	into	she
we	be	they	are
my	was	have	so
to	go	he	
me	you	all	
her	said	like	

Answers

Pages 6 to 7

Page 8

1. h**a**t
2. b**o**x
3. b**a**g
4. l**o**g
5. b**i**n
6. b**a**t

Page 9

1. Rubble can d**i**g it!
2. No job is too b**i**g, no p**u**p is too small!
3. Cali the c**a**t cannot st**o**p!
4. P**u**t it in the b**i**n!

Page 11

1. Rocky can **sit**.
2. Will Chase **catch** it?
3. Skye can **kick** it.
4. Jump, Marshall, **jump**!

Pages 12 to 13

Page 16

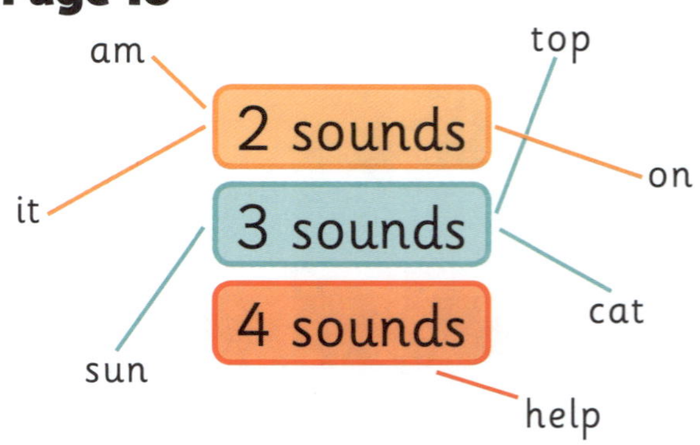

Page 17

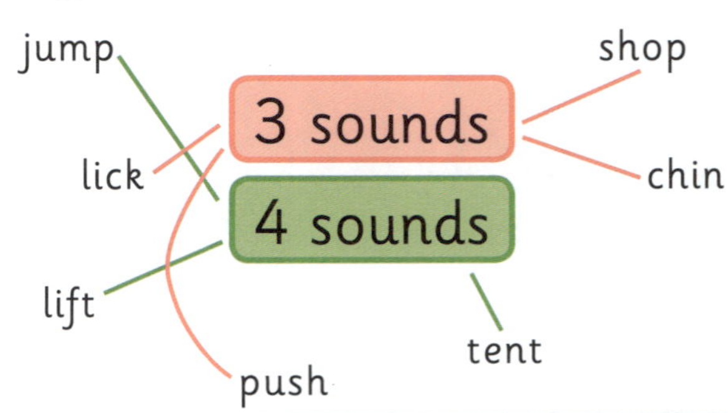

Page 19

Page 20

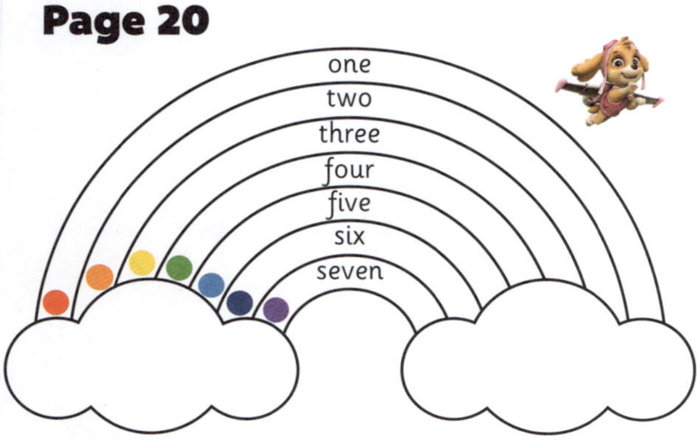

Page 22

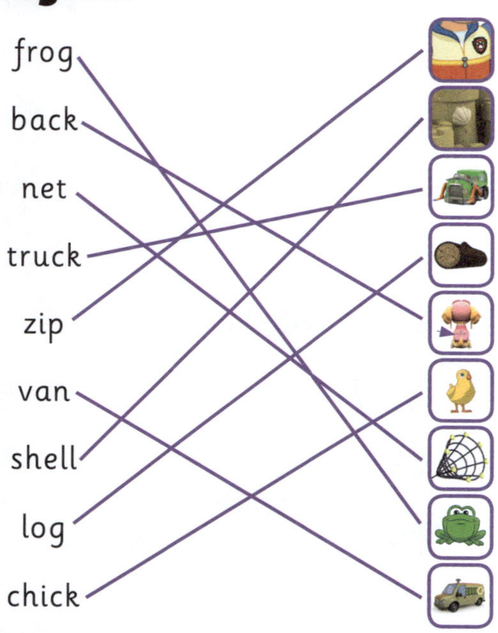

Page 23

frog
back
net
truck
zip
van
shell
log
chick

Page 24

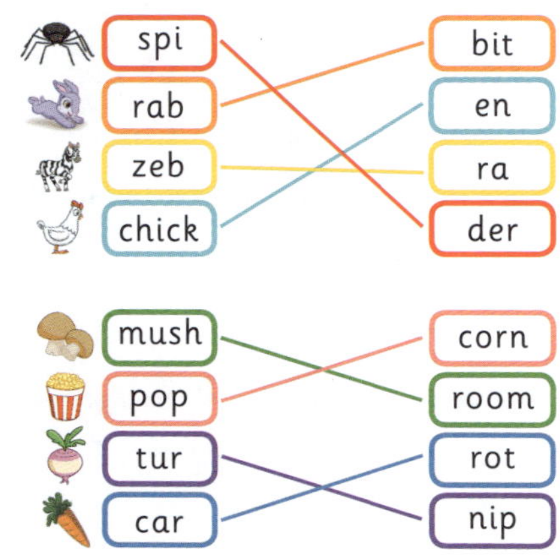

Page 25

1	hel met (circled)	helm et
2	tra iners	train ers (circled)
3	han dbag	hand bag (circled)
4	jac ket	jack et (circled)
5	jet pack (circled)	jetpa ck
6	skate board (circled)	ska teboard
7	toyb ox	toy box (circled)
8	footb all	foot ball (circled)

Answers

Page 26

word	long a sound	short a sound
wait	✓	
bang		✓
tail	✓	
aim	✓	
black		✓
stamp		✓
sail	✓	
train	✓	
hand		✓
cat		✓

Page 27

word	long e sound	short e sound
peg		✓
sleep	✓	
bed		✓
leg		✓
deep	✓	
feel	✓	
pen		✓
keep	✓	
see	✓	
sheep	✓	

Pages 28 to 29

1. Start at the gr**ee**n tr**ee**.
2. Follow the direction of Rocky's t**ai**l.
3. What can Chase s**ee**? It's a b**ee**.
4. Head towards the tr**ai**n.
5. Cr**ee**p past one pup fast asl**ee**p.
6. Well done! You have found the lost sh**ee**p.

Page 30

word	long i sound	short i sound
kick		✓
night	✓	
fish		✓
hill		✓
fit		✓
high	✓	
light	✓	
bin		✓
right	✓	
sigh	✓	

Page 31

word	long o sound	short o sound
dot		✓
job		✓
sock		✓
road	✓	
goat	✓	
pocket		✓
float	✓	
goat	✓	
hot		✓
coat	✓	

Page 32

Page 33

1. Let's dig it!
2. Green means go!
3. I can swing it!
4. Ready, set, get wet!
5. Time for a ruff-ruff rescue!

Page 34

word	long oo sound	short u sound
roof	✓	
food	✓	
mud		✓
bucket		✓
moon	✓	
sun		✓
bug		✓
zoom	✓	
cool	✓	
pup		✓

Page 35

ar car jar star (train) barn
or corn (moon) worn fork shorts
ow cow brown (float) down owl

Page 40

hardhat
tugboat
sweetcorn
balloon
trainers
toolbox
lightbulb
rainbow

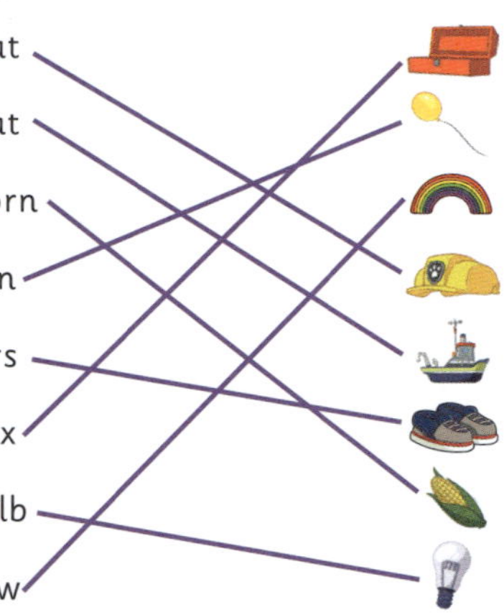

Page 41

trainers hardhat
balloon toolbox
rainbow tugboat
sweetcorn lightbulb

nickelodeon

PAW PATROL

CONGRATULATIONS!

....

(Name)

has completed the PAW Patrol Workbook:

FIRST SPELLING

Ages 4–5

Presented on:

....

(Date)

....

(Parent's signature)